Real Estate Investing

For Beginners

Make money investing in real estate and generate passive income, wealth, and financial freedom (with flipping, commercial or rental property, and realty business ideas).

Jordan Priesley

TABLE OF CONTENTS

Introduction

If you are an adult who pays bills, one idea reigns supreme in your mind all the time; it is the thought of how to earn more and become wealthy. We all want to attain a certain level of wealth because it makes it easier for us to do the things we desire. So the question we consistently ask ourselves is this, "How can I make more money?"

While there are numerous businesses, jobs and careers you can utilise to make money, there is one avenue that guarantees timeless wealth you can pass on to future generations. I'm talking about INVESTMENTS IN REAL ESTATE.

The concept of wealth shouldn't be about what you can do to make money for that moment, but how to pool your resources together to guarantee long-term income. So, our focus should be on how to secure more opportunities for passive income.

The objective of this book is to guide beginners through the pathway to get the most out of real estate investment. The chapters and sections you will find below are replete with information that will inspire you to take chances and do more with what you earn.

When the objective of this book is fulfilled, you will experience what it means to be genuinely financially free. Sometimes, economic freedom seems like an illusion for some people who have tried to attain it. You can enjoy economic freedom in the real estate space if you apply the right principles.

The pathway to the right principles includes an application of this equation: MINDSET + KNOWLEDGE = WEALTH. Knowledge of how to transform your finances combined with a change in mind-set awaits you in the sections you will read through. True lasting wealth is possible; it all begins with the acquisition of knowledge.

The process of investing in real estate goes beyond buying and selling houses; there are many concepts to unbox and learn. It all begins with the first chapter, which focuses on real estate as the pathway to sustainable wealth.

Ready to read through the very first chapter? Head over there now!

Chapter One

Real Estate: The Pathway to Sustainable Wealth

There has been a real estate boom that has caused a lot of people to refocus their attention on the market, and now more people are aware of the authenticity of wealth via real estate proceeds. But, is this boom enough to create sustainable wealth?

When we speak of wealth that is sustainable, we refer to long-lasting and impactful wealth that transcends generations. What else will make for sustainable wealth if not homes and land properties?

Come on, look around you; everywhere you turn, there is a house. We live, survive, and connect based on what we have as properties. The thought of being able to make money off real estate ought to make you extremely excited, because it has great rewards.

More than ever today, more people are attempting to become real estate moguls, and all of them strive to use techniques that will work for them. This has led to a surge in the number of books on real estate. However, it is advisable that you join the wagon with wisdom.

Real estate markets are known for being unstable. As such, every investor (novice or experienced) must become conversant with the principles of successful investing before going ahead with any investment plans.

Without a doubt, the real estate market is beautiful, because when you do make a profit over outstanding sales, it is always a good one. Unlike other sectors in which you may be unsure about the status of your investment despite challenging times, one thing is sure; properties always sell!

So, if you invest in some properties, it is possible to hold off on selling them until you find the right buyer who offers a great price. Should anything happen to a property or investor (accidents or death), the family of that investor can reap a neat profit from the property or pass it on to future generations.

I want you to know that you are on the right path in your search for true, lasting wealth. But, there is a lot of work to be done and many concepts to learn, first.

I always like to share the story of Zuri, a close friend who utilised the ideas shared in this book to make her first real estate investment move. At the time Zuri implemented what she learned, this book wasn't even in print; I just shared the ideas with her and boom! - she put them to work.

Zuri had to follow through with all the ideas we had discussed. She recognised the importance of matching the ideas with actions (which is so essential). And, five years later, Zuri is the proud owner of 12 properties.

I know you are imagining how much she's going to make already with twelve properties, but the number of features isn't the main attraction with this story. What I love about Zuri's story is the fact that she was able to turn those action plans into a success story. It really wouldn't matter if it were just one property she secured; what matters is the fact that with focus and a determined mind, she achieved and surpassed her goals.

So - why real estate? Why should anyone rely on real estate as a source of passive income? Read on to get answers.

The Benefits of Real Estate for Wealth Creation

1. It is a sure means for passive income.

Passive income is money you gain without having to go to work every day; it is money you don't actively work for. As such, it is the best form of income anyone could aspire to enjoy. You are not considered wealthy until you have a lot of avenues for passive income.

Wealth shouldn't be something you struggle to achieve, nor should it be something that makes you work too hard. You should just put in the work, and it should yield the right results; this is what real estate offers you.

2. Properties always appreciate.

Regardless of how challenging it will be, properties will still appreciate. This is one advantage of real estate investment that makes it very appealing. Zuri isn't bothered about the state of her properties because she knows that whenever she is ready to sell, she will make a profit.

Several investment platforms have a cloud of uncertainty around them; their volatile nature makes it increasingly difficult for people to enjoy the dividends of their investments. An excellent example of such uncertain investments is stocks and shares. But with real estate, you won't have to deal with such issues - especially now that you have this definitive guide with you.

3. Diversification leads to stability.

Real estate diversifies your investment portfolio. This is good, but what is even more interesting is the fact that it can also lead to security in your collection.

When you become an investor, you shouldn't seek assets in just one sector; you can diversify and do more with what you have through various channels.

With real estate, your portfolio is broadened. You experience stability, because when other investments are unstable, your properties bring in a balance that strengthens the portfolio. This feature of real estate investment is crucial to wealth creation.

4. Increased cash flows.

Due to increase in values, your cash flows will also experience the same growth. You have the choice to increase prices on your property and match it up with the current price in the market, and this gives you access to cash whenever you want it.

In a chapter ahead, we will be dealing with the concept of being a landlord. That chapter throws further insight into how real estate aids cash flow. Before we get to that section, you should know that real estate investments will increase your cash flow.

5. Title ownership.

With real estate investment, you also get to enjoy the title ownership of properties. You OWN the properties and decide what you want to do with them. Some people get into severe financial trouble and search for assets to sell off to fix their issues. Yet, because they do not own anything, they are unable to help themselves.

If you invest in real estate, you will have an opportunity to win something that increases in value over time. The most remarkable feeling that wealth gives you is the knowledge of being able to get what you need when you need it; this is a summary of how valuable real estate can be.

6. Transferrable wealth.

Some investments are not transferrable; and this has enormous implications for people who want to invest for their families, spouses, kids, and other third parties.

However, real estate is transferrable. That means you can invest today and transfer the property with its value to another person. It is safe to say that investment in real estate is the gift that keeps on giving; it is a perfect gift idea for someone you love.

More importantly, the fact that it is transferrable also means you can create a legacy of wealth others can build on for a very long time.

7. Tax benefits.

It is possible to get tax deductions on your mortgage interest as you invest in real estate. The tax deductions also apply to cash flows from investment properties, operating expenses, and costs. Insurance and depreciation are not left out in tax deductions.

So, when you start investing, you might want to wrap up all your deals before the year runs out. The end of the year is always a busy time for real estate, as it is an opportunity to utilise all the tax benefits.

With investments in real estate, there are no actual losses; you may have the occasional experiences that every investor has with a stake, but there is one sure thing; you will make a profit.

Over the years, the real estate industry has grown in value as everyone is trying to get their hands on it. You have reached the advantage over everyone else because you are armed with the right tools, knowledge, and information on how this works. So, be prepared to win and get ready to achieve a whole lot with this book.

Since there is an ever-increasing appeal with the real estate market, so many people jump right in and expect instantaneous results. When the results don't pour in as expected, they become frustrated and term the real estate sector "DIFFICULT." Well, I don't think Zuri would have made the kind of progress she did if she had not been patient. Five years is a long time - and Zuri had to wait.

So, in a bid to show you the importance of waiting, we will be heading right over to the next chapter, which will teach you all about the pitfalls of the "get-rich-quick" approach. It is an enlightening chapter that will lead us right into the central conversations of how to invest and succeed with real estate.

Chapter Two

Avoiding the "Get-Rich-Quick" Approach

L asting wealth takes time to grow; every successful person who shares their story with you will tell you that it took a lot of time for them to arrive at the level of success they now enjoy. The same principle applies to real estate investment.

If you are going to reap the rewards of this approach to investment, then you must get rid of the "get-rich-quick" method. In this chapter, we will consider what the approach is and proffer solutions on how you can be refocused on your investment goals without expecting instant results.

For a person to build wealth quickly, they must do things slowly. There has to be a process of thinking before action is taken. This process helps you weigh all options, thus clearing the pathway for increased success with your investment.

A lot of investors are lured into real estate because they see how many other people excel at it; what they fail to recognise and apply is the fact that these successful people invest an equal amount of time and effort to ensuring that they accomplish their set goals.

For some other successful investors, it was just pure luck.

So if you are considering winning with your real estate investment portfolio, you have to be ready to work on it long term. Those who try to achieve success at once are often disappointed, frustrated, and lose the motivation to continue with their investment.

Simply put - there are no shortcuts to succeeding with real estate. You must imbibe two principles for long-term success; and they are **patience** and **hard work**. Some investors learn a new trick and instantly want to use it to reach the peak. After a few weeks, they realise it won't work and must start all over again.

Some other investors observe a pattern of successful investors and apply it, albeit in a common way. The point is, if you do not put in the same effort, you will not get the same results. The sooner you get the idea of "get-rich-quick" out of your mind, the better off you'll be.

Real estate is like weight loss; everyone talks about it, a lot of people try to make it work, but only a few experience the effects of weight loss. There are millions of people in the real estate and weight loss industry, but only a few get to the peak.

With weight loss, you are told to do straightforward things such as exercise and eat fruits and vegetables, yet the process itself isn't simple. Anyone who has tried to lose weight will tell you it is a serious challenge; it is so severe that some people give up midway into their weight loss programs. In the midst of the struggle, some people come on television to testify about the effect of the process in their lives.

So, sitting in your home and watching those testimonials will cause you to wonder if there is something you are doing wrong. The weight loss experience isn't a fraudulent one; you are just not putting in the required effort and work needed; and until you do, your weight will be a struggle.

Too many people are impatient; it is the reason they don't get the results they seek. If you are serious about losing weight, the same way you are passionate about succeeding in real estate, you will follow through with the process regardless of how long it takes.

There are some steps you can take toward ensuring that your philosophy about real estate doesn't deviate to the "get-rich-quick" pattern. Below, you will find the steps you should consider.

How to Achieve Real Estate Investment Plans

1.   Set realistic goals.

First, you must have goals. For anything significant to succeed, you must have a plan - and your goals form the springboard of your projects. So, if you are prepared to succeed, you have to sit still and curate plans that focus on how you want to execute your real estate business.

With your goals in hand, you will have a compass that drives and propels you forward - even in challenging times. Before you launch out to begin your real estate adventure, take the time to set goals.

2. Work hard.

Now, the importance of this cannot be overemphasised. You must work hard to ensure that your goals come to fruition. Your goals give you the motivation you hope for the future, but hard work is what makes a dream come true.

Every day, do something that takes you closer to the realisation of your goals. For every effort you make, you will be rewarded with success. So, work hard and put in your best work toward your goals.

3. Be patient.

As you curate goals and work hard, remember to exercise patience. Do not be in a hurry to get results, because impatience makes people miss out on something good. You should imbibe the culture of tolerance that enables you to hold on to something until it works out for you.

Tell yourself you are not going to give up until the results start to trickle in. An investor who wants to succeed must be patient; this is a rule that is true of all investment sectors.

4. Focus on quality, not quantity.

A lot of times, investors are in a hurry to excel. As such, they start buying properties. Oh! They buy a lot of features in a bid to show how "successful" they are. Going for quantity over quality is always the wrong approach.

Instead of buying many properties that aren't valuable, it is advisable that you stick with quality over quantity. It is better to have one house that is an asset positioned to increase in value within a specified period than have several properties that are undervalued. Always remember this; stick to quality over quantity.

5. Education + action = success.

Next, you need to educate yourself on the principles and steps to take for successful real estate investment. However, education is not enough; it is crucial that you match your education with actionable steps.

Education + action is the combination that leads to success as a real estate investor. So as much as you are committed to learning, be focused on acting as well. Everything you read, starting with this book, should come to life and work for you.

6. Continue learning

You must continue learning so you always have ways through which you can stay motivated and forget about the "get-rich-quick" pattern. If you had not read this book, you probably wouldn't have gotten all of the ideas you have now.

Read more books and continue to inspire yourself with words and plans. Books, mailing lists, podcasts, etc. are all avenues for learning you can utilize.

7. Aspire and emulate.

Don't just look up to others; make up your mind that you are going to be like them. So first, you must develop the aspirations to be like the successful investors you see - and then emulate them by putting in the same kind of work they put into their investments.

The pattern to success doesn't end with aspirations alone; act, fail, learn, fail, and continue until it is perfected.

8. Observe the trends.

Trends help us decipher what is working and what isn't. You must observe the real estate market, the same way you track your shares and stocks.

By not observing trends, you will be listening to speculations from non-investors - or unprofessional ones who want to get instant cash. Follow the pattern by following other original investors like yourself; you will get to know what's happening within seconds.

9. Avoid magic bullets.

Magic bullets refer to quick fixes people look for to succeed; they are not the steps that lead to sustainable wealth, nor are they the approaches that will lead to long-term success.

Magic bullets will make it difficult for you to see the bigger picture. As such, they must be avoided at all costs. Magic bullets make it all seem very easy; but in no time, it will come crashing down on you.

10.   Reach out to someone else.

They say the best way to learn on a deeper level is to teach what you know. If you recall Zuri's story, it will interest you to know that I gained a lot from her when she came back and said she had used my principles.

If you want all of these lessons to become a part of your long-term strategy, you need to find someone who is also willing to embark on this journey – and teach that person all you know. While sharing your ideas, you will also learn a thing or two.

Some people want to get involved with real estate one day and start making a lot of money the following day. This book is going to empower you to think differently. You can achieve all you desire; but first, there are things you must put in place to ensure that you are on the right path to success.

Follow the steps you've got above carefully, plan, and execute; you will be amazed at how far you go with your real estate investment. With real estate, some people think it is just about buying and selling houses. There are numerous ways through which you can generate wealth - and we are going to discover them in the next chapter.

Chapter Three

Numerous Ways to Build Wealth

There are one thousand and one different ways to build wealth, but when it comes to real estate, there are multiple distinct options. Real estate is not just buying and selling, as much as it is about having sustainable wealth through different avenues. This chapter will take you through all the numerous ways to build your wealth in real estate.

Generating wealth in real estate focuses on pooling all available resources and tapping opportunities to create the lasting wealth you desire. It is about knowing what works, applying it with the right timing, and having the patience to reap the benefits.

There are numerous, easy-to-follow, practical, and proven ways to build your wealth in real estate; but most importantly, you must ensure you have the determination, perseverance, and patience to pull it off. These three qualities are what distinguish the successful real estate investors from their less successful counterparts.

Zuri didn't only achieve her twelve property feat through these avenues, but with determination, perseverance and patience. You also can do the same and much more. Let's see the numerous ways to build your wealth in real estate.

1. Below Market Value Purchase

Buying and selling in real estate are only profitable when you buy at a low market price and sell at a high market price. It is the best way to maximise your profits. Certain conditions warrant the sales of a property below its market value. These conditions are the opportunities you must tap into as a real estate investor.

Some people who want to sell fast without hassle, lenders with foreclosures (REOs), and those that are misinformed about the market trends give rise to these opportunities. It is, however, vital to get your facts straight and not fall victim to investment frauds. Having the right, timely information can earn you a secured real estate investment below the market value.

This is a guarantee of generating lasting wealth.

2. The 'Appreciation' Effect

If you have been in existence for almost 3-4 decades, look around you; you can testify that things and times have changed. It is a known fact that in 5-10 years, there are changes in population, jobs, incomes, wealth, restrictions on development, immigration rates, construction costs, investors, and so on. These changes are on the high side known as the 'Appreciation' effect.

As a real estate investor, you should know that real estate properties tend to appreciate; the same goes for the factors that affect it. There will be population, jobs, income, and wealth increases as time goes by. And real estate properties will continue to appreciate. It means you can leverage on this fact to generate your wealth in real estate.

3. The Cash Flow System

In real estate, there is a belief that the primary source of cash flow is the rent - and it is true! The cash flow system allows you to use different factors to influence your cash flow. Inflation and an increase in market demand are such factors that can help boost your cash flows.

During inflation, interest rates are up, and you can generate more cash flow. As we progress further, we shall look at how you can manage your cash flow to help you create more wealth, so do read on.

4. Paying Off Your Mortgage through Amortisation

Investing in a mortgage is a secure avenue in real estate; the only tricky part is that while the property is in your name, its original owner can choose to retrieve it unless you pay it off. Amortisation is the process of paying off your mortgage with the rent collected on it. This is a means of generating more wealth.

Let's say you invest $10,000 in a mortgage worth $100,000; you pay it off with its rent after 20 years, you would have succeeded in acquiring a property worth ten times your investment and a 12 percent annual rate on the compound interest. This is pretty much a secured and guaranteed money-making venture in real estate.

5. Marketing for Profitability

What makes the difference in the business of real estate are the strategies and proper planning aimed at creating more profits after studying trends. A successful real estate investor is always on the lookout for positive trends in the market, new marketing strategies, and all it takes to generate more profits.

To achieve your goals of investing in real estate, you must be an effective marketer. Learn new strategies and study trends to generate more wealth.

6. The Value-Added Investment (VAI)

Have you ever seen a property that left you astonished and your jaws hitting the floor? There are many properties out there that are very different from their original architectural structures. As a real estate investor, calling more crowd would mean adding more value.

You can make cosmetic changes to your property, renovate it entirely, or give it the 'extra' features to increase your chances of attracting high-value customers. If you have a townhouse – turned - campsite, you can add a beautiful backyard to attract more customers.

We shall discuss how to increase the value of your property in a later chapter.

7. Maximising Inflation

Inflation is the decrease in the value of money due to the increase in the quantity of money in circulation. You may be wondering how inflation helps to generate more wealth in real estate. Here is how it works. When there is an increase in the amount of money in circulation, there is a price jump for properties, and rent increases - as well as interest rates.

You can maximise inflation by renting out your properties or selling them to the highest bidder at that time. You get to acquire more money during that period.

8. Enhancing the Neighbourhood

There are many popular neighbourhoods out there, and many real estate investors would love to invest there. Here is a secret for you; there are also many downtrodden and abandoned neighbourhoods that have the potential of being famous. Take your investment there, purchase at a low price, and sell when popular demand calls.

You also get to do the community a service by bringing development and civilisation to such neighbourhoods, which is a win-win situation for you.

9. Trending Conversions

An interesting fact about real estate is that it is a flexible field. It isn't limited to only one facet, and this gives it an advantage over other businesses. Conversions of properties based on trends and demand serve as a means of generating more wealth. A property can be converted into another based on its purpose.

If you have a property in a residential area which is fast becoming an industrial city, converting the apartment or home into an office building is a great way to generate more wealth. It is, however, important to study the trends and market demands before dabbling into such conversions.

10. Protection from Tax

You cannot build wealth when the government is swallowing your profits in the form of taxes. This is the reason you must put on the armour of protection to save your earnings. There are four ways to protect your profits from tax, and they are:

- **Depreciation:** This is the non-cash tax deduction on your properties. It is the tax paid on the remaining part of your property's net worth not generating income. It helps you minimise taxes paid.

- **Serial Home Selling:** This is another means of protecting your properties from tax. If you have a property in which you have resided for two years out of five, you can sell such property without paying tax. You can also keep reselling such properties every two years and not spend a single dime on tax.

- **Retirement Plans:** There are tax-favoured retirement plans you can invest in and use all proceeds to invest in your real estate business.

- **Section 1031:** Section 1031 of the internal revenue code permits you to sell a personal property tax-free in exchange for purchasing a new one within a stipulated time.

Other ways of building wealth in real estate include realty stocks, discounted notes, tax liens, tax deeds, and many more.

The above methods of building wealth in real estate are mainly discussed to assure you enjoy sustainable wealth in real estate. Once you have the money to start investing, the outcome is predictable with adequate planning. This brings us to raising money for investing in real estate. The next chapter goes into details on raising the money needed for your real estate investments. Do read and enjoy.

Chapter Four

Raising Money

H aving read up to this point, you will agree with me that we are getting there in regards to being educated and enlightened about real estate investments. This chapter is crucial as it teaches you how to raise money as a beginner in the real estate business. Read and learn more.

As popular as the demand for real estate investments is, having the money to invest - as well as the means of getting such money - is what matters. Real estate, unlike other businesses, requires a substantial amount of money to achieve success.

There are numerous means of raising money for real estate investments, but this chapter focuses on practical methods for beginners like you.

To make your money count, you must have the mindset of a farmer who cultivates rubber plants. The farmer knows that it will take him approximately six years to harvest the latex of the rubber plant, but remains undaunted and patiently waits while he does all necessary activities needed to produce his rubber tree and latex.

You must have the mindset that the money raised is the seed needed to yield the tree of sustainable wealth in real estate - and you must take all necessary measures to attain it.

The following are means of raising money for your real estate investments as a beginner:

1. Personal Funding

For anyone beginning the journey to financial freedom through real estate, this is the number one source of raising money for your investments. Personal funding refers to funding from your own pocket, using your savings, bonds, equity, mutual funds, and all other liquid assets. Personal funding saves you hassles from financial bodies, private investors, and other external contributors.

If you are good at sourcing for personal funds or you have family members and friends that can give you free money to start your real estate business, then you are good to go. This must, however, be done after setting goals and enumerating ways of achieving them.

Another method of personal funding is leasing your home out to start up and finance your real estate business. It is your home, and you can use the rent payments collected in refinancing your real estate business.

If you recall Zuri, my friend who got to follow all the principles in this book and ended up with a twelve property feat after five years, then let me tell you that Zuri started by leasing out all of the top floor rooms in her townhome. She converted her parents' room, the guest room, and the film room hall into a two bedroom apartment and leased it out as her first real estate investment.

You can start yours as Zuri did - or by buying a property with your funds to begin your real estate investment.

2. Other People's Funds

As a beginner, if you are short on cash or do not have any liquid assets to start your real estate investments with, here is an alternative - using other people's funds. This method of raising money may not be as easy as having your own funds; nevertheless, it doesn't seem all too bad. To achieve this feat, you must pay extra attention and learn the ropes of raising money from others.

No one would gladly invest in something without a certain percentage of guarantee that it would be successful. As a beginner, you must have SMART real estate investment goals that would convince the investors of their choice.

Having SMART investment goals is good, but most importantly, you must display a good sense of responsibility and be up front in your dealings. You may have people of good character validate that you have all it takes to invest wisely.

Other people's funds may include funds from private investors, creditors in the real estate business, private lenders, credit unions, bank loans, and so on. You can also be a middleman in the chain of distribution and use the money earned in refinancing your real estate investments.

You can engage in mortgage loans as well, and this is highly profitable as you can pay off the loan with the rent collected from the mortgage (amortisation, discussed earlier). Partnering with another trusted real estate beginner like yourself is also a great way of raising money for your real estate investments.

Of all of the above, a private investor is the best option as there are fewer protocols and requirements and more of friendliness, trust, and passion for succeeding to help make your real estate investments worthwhile.

3. Seller Funds

If you want to explore another facet of real estate known as Real Estate Wholesaling, this type of fundraising is what you should focus on as a beginner. Real estate wholesaling involves the scouting of potential and high-value buyers for sellers with properties and closing the deal. It is a middleman job and can help you raise money to finance your real estate investments.

With real estate wholesaling, you are preparing yourself to handle your own real estate investments while being exposed to the market trends and demands. This aspect of real estate requires negotiating and excellent communication skills. You must also be willing to sacrifice a lot of time and work twice as hard to please the seller.

This is how it works - you find a seller willing to sell fast and without corporate hassle, negotiate, and put into writing how you want him or her to fund the back work in getting a high-value buyer. Ensure any agreement made is documented and legalised to avoid future complications.

Then, you proceed to find interested and high-value buyers, give them a tour of the property, convince them to buy if it's a good deal for both sides, then close the deal. Make your own money and finance your real estate business. Easy, right? Just ensure you have adequate knowledge and avoid real estate investments scams.

Raising money for your real estate investments isn't as hard as it seems; it only requires your determination, perseverance, and patience to make it work. With the money raised through any of the above means, you can now proceed to invest in your real estate business. The next chapter will discuss how to handle your real estate business. Watch out for practical guides and tips.

Chapter Five

Real Estate is a Business - Handle it That Way

A real estate business is not different from an 8-4 job. A banker with a dream of being the Chairman of the Board of a big financial institution will start from scratch and work his/her way to the top. They would work hard, attend conferences, be on their best behaviour, and seek out promotions - all in a bid to achieve that dream. All other things being equal, with enough hard work, determination, and consistency, such a goal would come to pass.

A business should be treated more or less in the same way. Every successful business owner can attest to the fact that they had to manage the business as a priority and sacrifice a lot to achieve their dreams. Real estate is a business; hence, it must be handled as such. This chapter will educate you, as a beginner, on how to handle your real estate investments like a business.

Many real estate investors often see the real estate field as another side money-making venture; this has helped to distinguish the successful ones from others.

Real estate investments are not different from other businesses out there, and to become successful at it, you must be able to handle it as such.

These practical guides and tips for handling your real estate investments as a business are genuine and have been tested to yield quality results. These guides and tips were borne out of experience and lessons learned along the way of real estate investments.

It is essential you read and digest this chapter well, as this will take you to your desired goal of sustainable wealth through real estate.

Practical guides and tips on how to handle your real estate investments as a business:

1. Invest your full time.

As said earlier, many real estate investors often go into it with a mindset of a part-time venture. This has, however, not yielded the desired results. Since business isn't different from a day job – and real estate is a business - you should invest your full time in it. Full-time investments will enable you to focus and achieve optimal sustainability.

As a full-time real estate investor, you get to work with flexibility and achieve great results. You can answer calls at any time, get inspiration and ideas at any time, and make crucial decisions any time. You also get to learn a lot due to your full commitment and don't end up as a "Jack of all trades." Investing full time will allow you to pursue your real estate investment goals relentlessly.

Tip: If you can't invest your full time due to your job as you are depending on its stable income - or for any other reasons, do invest part-time. This only means you have to work twice as hard, be diligent and goal-oriented, multitask, and have a support structure.

The support structure could be your winning team (will be discussed later as one of the guides in handling your real estate business), your friends, or other reliable real estate investors you know. If you are into real estate business as a retirement plan, you must also invest quality time to achieve your goals. Real estate is a long term business, and it is like sowing a rubber seed to yield a rubber tree after many efforts and much time.

2. Set goals and plan ahead
There are no two ways about it; you must set goals and plan ahead. A business only thrives when specific goals are set and proper planning is ensured to meet the set goals. Everyone talks about setting goals, but how many do? As a beginner in real estate, you must avoid being like such people and set realistic goals.

Why should you set goals and plan for your real estate business? You must be able to define your purpose to achieve your desires. The setting of goals will require prioritising your needs and wants. It will also allow you to highlight the means of achieving them. This process will point out measurable milestones and ways forward.

There are short term and long term goals in real estate. Short term goals, as the name implies, refer to goals that are set to be achieved within a short amount of time. These short term goals also serve as milestones for long term goals. Examples of short term goals include leasing out part or all of your home, finding buyers for a property within some months, owning a property from a year's rent, and so on. These goals are achievable within their stipulated time frame.

Long term goals are goals set to be achieved in a long while. These goals are what you aim to accomplish over time with your real estate business. Long term goals are goals to be achieved in three to five years time. Examples include owning up to 10 properties in five years, being able to sustain yourself and your family with your business, setting up a real estate consulting firm, and so on. Long term goals may take time to be achieved, but through persistence, hard work, and determination, you can make it.

How to Set SMART Real Estate Goals

Define your goals regarding needs and time: Your goals have to be specific and time-bound; hence, you have to define them regarding needs and time. For instance, Zuri's short term goal was to own a rental home after a year of leasing out a part of her townhome. This is an example of defining your goals regarding your needs and time. You may want something similar or something slightly different. Ensure they are realistic and achievable. Do not go overboard.

- **Prioritize your goals in order of importance:** What makes your goals SMART is the order of importance attached to them. In as much as you are working toward sustainable wealth through real estate business, your goals must be arranged in order of what is most important.

- **Analyse your goals for actualization:** This is a critical step in setting goals. You must analyse your defined goals to ensure that you can actualize them. Your goals must be realistic and achievable. You should set your goals based on your actual and potential resources. You should also look at your level of availability and commitment. Don't forget to factor external factors like economic situation, rules and laws, and other people that would be involved.

- **Evaluate often:** Now this may sound futuristic, but that's what it is. As you progress in your real estate business, ensure you make evaluations as you achieve your set goals. This allows you to set further goals or redefine your already set goals, depending on the progress status. This brings you to planning ahead of time and salvaging distressful situations.

Planning allows you to foresee any future losses as well as setbacks. Proper planning ensures adequate success in all your endeavors. It goes without saying that you must set goals and plan toward achieving them to succeed in your real estate business.

Tip: Since this is the jet age, you can make use of computer software to organise your goals, plans, and achievements. GoldMine, Microsoft Outlook, and ACT are examples of software programs you can employ.

3. Have the right attitude toward work.

For your real estate business to thrive, you need to have the right attitude toward work. Treat your real estate business the same way you would treat any other business - or rather how you would go about your office career. Attitude is everything; the right attitude toward work can help you land great deals, and can make the right impression on an investor. You must ensure you are at your best at all times.

Attitude to Portray in the Real Estate Business:

- **Be punctual:** Time is an essential factor in being successful. Many significant deals and connections have been lost as a result of not keeping to time. As a beginner in the real estate business, you must ensure you keep to time.

When you schedule a meeting with your client, ensure you get there at least five minutes beforehand. You should also call ahead when you can't meet up with deadlines. This shows professionalism and discipline.

- **Be diligent:** Hard work plus consistency equals diligence. As a beginner in the real estate business, you can't afford to be less than diligent in your activities. Follow your plans accordingly, gather necessary information, be consistent, and strive to do your best. Diligence is the key to a successful business.

- **Dress appropriately:** As almost insignificant as this may seem, it is imperative. Your looks define who you are, so if you are aspiring to be a CEO, dress the part.

- **Pay attention to details:** Paying attention to details is a great trait you can develop with conscious effort. This attitude is necessary in the real estate business. Being observant to all things can help you from falling into investments scams and frauds.

Tip: You should also be friendly and approachable as a beginner - but don't let your guard down. Everyone should see you as their go-to real estate investor, but you shouldn't be taken for granted. Note that it is crucial you separate business from pleasure to ensure professionalism.

4. Put together your winning team.

You are a winner; and your team is a vital part of ensuring your success in the real estate business. As a beginner, it is imperative you put together a team of competent and reliable people that can assure you of a smooth sail through your real estate business. These professionals must be experienced in their respective fields and be available to be of help when needed.

Your winning team should include:

- **A good real estate attorney:** You must hire or consult not any real estate attorney - but a good one. You need an attorney with enough knowledge about real estate to advise you about the risks and help you secure a great deal. He or she must also be able to suggest other practical transaction alternatives and be frank with you about your investments. Having a good attorney that can charge a reasonable fee is also an advantage.
- **A competent title company:** A title company is in charge of closing deals. To ensure a smooth closing, consult a qualified title company. Find a small and reliable company that caters to investors. Look into recommendations from trusted and successful real estate investors.
- **An experienced tax advisor:** One of the advantages of investing in real estate is having it easy when it comes to taxes. A qualified tax advisor will give practical advice on how to cut taxes and acquire as little as possible. An

experienced tax advisor will also help in preparing the tax to pay from your business. Ensure you have adequate knowledge on whom to hire.

- **A handy contractor:** if you are trying to invest in 'conversions' or other rehabilitative types of real estate business, you need a helpful contractor. You need someone that is readily available to fix things within your proposed budget. A handy contractor must also be knowledgeable about trends and have the capacity to turn scraps into wonders. Hire a helpful contractor you can trust.

- **A mortgage broker:** Consulting a mortgage broker is necessary when investing in mortgages. It is essential you do your homework correctly before entrusting a mortgage broker with your business. Ask questions about those that have benefitted from their services. Ask for references and qualifications to prove competence and reliability.

- **A mentor:** As a beginner, it is vital you have someone that mentors you in the real estate business. You need a knowledgeable, reliable, and trustworthy mentor to guide through building your real estate business. You must also understand that this person has their own life to live, so tread with caution.

Tip: You can go into partnership in your real estate venture. Be an active partner and contribute adequately. You should also respect your partner's opinions and contributions. Learn diplomacy skills to enable you to make joint decisions.

5. Procure all necessary tools to the trade.

A business needs the right tools to function. You must gather information on the required tools needed to operate your real estate business smoothly. The tools required depend on the aspects of real estate you are considering. This book will discuss the essential tools needed as a beginner in the real estate business.

Essential tools to procure for your real estate business are:

- **An office with office essentials:** An office is vital for transactions and planning for your business. You can keep financial documents and hold crucial meetings or conference calls there. Necessary office essentials like a printer, photocopier, stapler, fax machine, a landline, printing paper, computer, and so on should also be procured. You can rent an office or use a room in your home as one.
- **Business cards:** These are essential to promote your real estate business. As a beginner, you may not be able to afford to make corporate cards; color business cards are affordable. You need to grow your connections; hence, your business cards must be professional and tell your story.

Include the necessary information and you can even make them two-sided.

- **A website:** This is also important to reach out to your virtual clients and propagate your business to the world. If you are skilled in web development, then you can do it yourself. If you are not, you can seek the service of a freelance web developer on freelancing sites like Fiverr, Freelancer, and so on, at a very affordable price.

- **A Retrieval system:** There are times you are just not available and vital messages may come in. To avoid regrets for missing out on those messages, it is advisable that you purchase an answering machine. This will enable you to record the messages you have missed and then act on them.

Tip: Other tools you can indulge in are social media platforms, a business mail, wireless phone, and a PC or laptop. It is crucial you don't overdo it; don't forget you have to manage your cash flow.

6. Increase efficiency through recruitment.

As time goes on and your business progresses positively, you may need to recruit office staff. These staff members can include a receptionist, a secretary, and/or an assistant that will help to take some work off your shoulders. Hiring competent and trusted individuals is vital.

You can recruit people recommended by trusted individuals or search for your own. Do background checks to ensure you don't hire a criminal. You may not have the budget to hire extra hands, but you can employ multitaskers and people that are willing to see your business through to greater heights.

Hire people that can key into your business dreams and won't treat your business lightly.

Tip: You can hire one person to do all office work. That is, such a person will be the receptionist/secretary. You can also recruit another person to assist you in your field work and deal scouting; this person may serve as your right-hand man or woman.

7. Know the rules and abide by them.

Rules and laws are essential, and as a law-abiding citizen, you must ensure you identify these rules and abide by them. In real estate, knowing the rules is essential to close deals properly, make a proper foreclosure, record your transactions well, and create good contracts. Laws vary depending on location and jurisdiction; hence, you must know the local rules of where you want to invest.

You also need rules in the form of tenancy agreements to lease out your properties without consequences. As a beginner, don't be ignorant; ask questions so you don't get into trouble for what could be avoided. Below is a list of rules you need to know about in the real estate business.

- **Tenancy rules:** If you are aspiring to own properties you will lease out, then you need to have in-depth knowledge about tenancy. You must learn about the laws that bind you as a landlord with your tenants in that area. You should also know the clauses surrounding evictions, security deposits, and rentals. Visit the housing office in the secretariat located in that area for more information.

- **Inspections:** This is a critical step in buying or selling a property. Traditionally, an inspection is done after the property is under a contract. This gives an opportunity to those wanting to cut out of the deal using the excuse of finding a reason during inspection to do so. As a seller, you can ask for an inspection before drafting a contract to avoid unnecessary delays.

- **Recording rules:** For every transaction affecting your real estate business, you must make a record at the county office. You must learn the laws surrounding recordings such as the fees, deed, transfer tax, document sizes, and the legalizing of such recording. These rules differ from county to county within a particular state.

- **Choosing a closing agent:** While it is believed that it is the seller who gets to choose the title company for closing a deal, the buyer gets the chance as well. You can request a closing agent of your choice as a buyer.

- **Foreclosure deals:** It is in your best interest to learn about the rules guiding a foreclosure deal. There are technical details you need to know about a foreclosure deal before you can trade in it. Ensure you have the right knowledge about it to avoid your transaction being nullified. Foreclosure rules differ from state to state, so take note of that.

- **Contract rules:** To ensure an official contract is drafted, you must learn the rules guiding it. Always insist on a formal draft to avoid legal issues. It isn't compulsory, but it helps you avoid legal problems.

Tip: Create a rapport with the locals where you want to invest, and ask them for help regarding those rules and how you can invest better. You can also log into the official website of the state to learn more about the rules or contact them to make enquires.

8. Secure great deals.

As important as bringing in money is to your real estate business, securing great deals is more important. As a beginner in the real estate business, the euphoria of bringing in more cash is always there. However, it is better when you can secure critical and significant deals that will open up constant cash flow for your business.

Spend your time and money on marketing and scouting for lucrative deals. You can even partner with investors to secure those deals if you are low on cash. That one property you let go of to secure more deals will pave the way in acquiring more properties.

Tip: Learn about your weaknesses and strengths in managing a business. This will open your eyes to how to secure better deals. Leverage your strengths and work on your weaknesses to secure great deals for your real estate business.

As you can deduce from the above, real estate is a business and must be handled as such. The guides are practical and easy to follow. The tips are the unique secrets you would need to guarantee your success as a real estate investor.

Real estate business must be practiced defensively. The next chapter will discuss what defensive investing is all about and the principles guiding it. Do read and learn more.

Chapter Six

Principles of Defensive Investing

In the previous chapter, you learned how to handle your real estate investments as a business, things to avoid, and tips to help you build your business. This chapter will focus on your real estate business as a defensive investment and the principles of defensive investing. You will learn what it means to invest defensively - be prepared to learn essential concepts here.

Defensive investing is the act of putting in money, hard work, and effort, gathering information and data, and managing your cash flows safely and securely to limit losses and avoid business setbacks. It is an indisputable fact that as an investor, you would prefer to create more wealth with the least risk through your real estate business.

Defensive investing allows you to focus on ways to limit your losses by avoiding investment scams and frauds, being part of unprofitable or shady deals, and investing at the wrong time. All these are what real estate investors take into consideration before venturing into the real estate world. If you are ready to invest defensively, ask yourself the following questions:

Am I prepared to create sustainable wealth through real estate?

Can I do all it takes to ensure I meet my set goals in achieving sustainable wealth?

Will I be able to stick it through until the end?

Once you can answer these questions, then you can proceed to learn about the principles that will guide you to invest defensively and create sustainable wealth through real estate. The following are the ten principles of defensive investing:

1. Have a long-term mind-set.

If you recall the second chapter of this book, which talked about avoiding the 'get-rich-quick' approach, this principle is very similar to that. Having a long-term mindset is necessary to invest defensively. You should have it at the back of your mind that you are sowing the seeds of a rubber tree or trying a weight loss plan.

You should note that both processes take a long while to see the results. Hence, you must be patient and focused to gain your desired results. Invest with the mindset of getting the dividends in the long run. You must nurture and train yourself to expect long-term effects. Avoid the 'get-rich-quick' approach with sought after, practical ways to achieve your sustainable wealth goals.

2. Timely information is key.

They say knowledge is power, but having the right expertise at the right time is wealth. To create wealth through real estate, you must always seek the correct information at the right time. It is crucial you have the right information - which is possessed at the right time - to secure a deal, to avoid losses and investment scams, and to own the right property at the right time.

Read books, seek advice, take courses, watch videos, and so on while engaging in a real estate business. This book is an excellent piece of information you have in your possession. Is it the right time?

You must also be reachable so that significant deals don't pass you by. Learn about the trends and markets. Be attentive and observant to notice changes that may affect your business.

3. Know your numbers.

As a real estate investor, you must know your real estate numbers to buy and sell correctly. There are seasons in the real estate business - and knowing them will help you know when to deal and when not to deal.

When market prices become low, you should know that buying will favor you at this point. You should also know when demands are high and the costs of properties are high.

Investing in a defensive manner means you must know all your numbers to maximize your gains and minimize your losses.

4. Buy, after calculating your profit.

Many times, losses are incurred after purchasing a property without digging into the profitability. As a beginner in the real estate business, always calculate your benefits first before buying any property.

You may be asking asking how you would know the profit on a long-term investment; it is simple. Be it a rental, a mortgage, or a property, it must fall into one of these to secure such deals:

- You can purchase it at a lesser price than its current market price.
- It can be converted and made into something better and much more valuable than its present state.
- It will provide sustainable income above its buying price.
- It will appreciate in a future market.

If your deal falls within any of those four categories, then be assured that you have a profitable deal; so act on it. A good deal can also vary from place to place, so ensure you have your facts straight to invest defensively.

5. Being 'safe' is paramount.

Being defensive in dealing means being safe in your investments. As a beginner, you should know that not all deals are secured and will lead to creating sustainable wealth. Some contracts have too high of a risk, and at the end of the day, may drive to huge losses. As a defensive investor, you must avoid that at all costs.

Learn what a good deal is; which is buying at a low price and selling at a high rate with enough profit to generate sustainable wealth.

A safe deal is a good deal with extra caution on things diving off to a wrong destination. This means regardless of how good the deal is, if it would cost you more to maintain than its proposed profits, then it isn't going to work.

For instance, fixer-uppers are known to be good deals, but for you as a beginner, you have to investigate to be sure such a deal isn't a waste of time. You need to seek the service of a professional to evaluate the property and notify you of its worth before dealing. You must ensure that any rehabilitative work done to fix the property won't consume too much of or waste your time and money.

Defensive investing involves being safe at all times. Even when there are risks to take, ensure the chances are low enough to be combatted as a beginner.

6. **Manage your cash flows.**

Every successful real estate investor refers to their cash flow; this shows how important the term is in the business of real estate. It is essential you understand how to operate and manage your cash flow as a defensive strategy of investing.

Having the right information on how to manage your cash flow is essential. How to determine the cash flowing for you in your real estate business is also vital to the success of your business.

As a beginner, it is advisable to have more cash reserves to avoid lending from banks or financial bodies. It is also advisable you keep cash with you and coming in, rather than pouring it all on some property. Several unforeseen matters arise unexpectedly; your cash flow can take care of such issues and still run your business smoothly. Hence, manage it wisely!

7. **Know ways to exit.**

Being defensive involves conscious effort to invest in safe deals and incur minimal losses. There are times when, despite all caution, things don't turn out as expected. When such results are discovered early, it is best to use an exit strategy to salvage the situation.

Exiting from a deal may occur as a result of blind deals with no profits or potential losses. It is vital to learn the ways to exit such agreements. Several exit options exist depending on the situation.

A chapter in this book will discuss in details the various options of exit strategies available. This will enlighten you on how to salvage some risky situations.

8. Earning it is right, keeping it is important.

What makes the difference in your defensive investments is whether you can hold on to your acquired wealth without any issues. Many real estate investors do battle with lawsuits and other problems that may allow them to end up losing their property or going bankrupt.

It is crucial you learn how to keep your wealth. Avoid shady deals that may come back to haunt you. Learn to keep records of all your activities and transactions. It is safe to say that learning about the several real estate rules, and abiding by them, will also help you secure your wealth.

Get educated on other investors' legal mistakes and how taxes work to avoid trouble with the law and authority. Be sure to go through the right and proper process of buying a property, leasing out a property, selling a property, or making deals.

It is vital to insure all your properties so as to keep them safe and not incur as many losses during setbacks like disasters, fire outbreaks, and so on. Insurance is key - and it defends you as an investor. Don't acquire lots of liabilities as an investor; secure your properties with good insurance policies.

Setting up a corporation or LLC can also protect you from acquiring liabilities as an investor. As your business continues to expand and grow, it would be safer to set up a corporate entity that would protect them all.

Earn your wealth, but also learn to keep it well to avoid wasting all the effort you put into it. Don't say "I was not aware." The same way you acquired the wealth, you can quickly lose it. Secure your wealth through the above plans and more from what you've learned.

9. Don't fall for investment scams

This is another means of keeping your hard-earned wealth. Many people are out there looking for those to defraud; and if you aren't careful, you may fall victim. Several real estate investors are after fast deals; hence, they fall victim of enticing and appealing fake deals. They cry foul, not knowing they allowed themselves to be swayed by the sweet words and fraudulent deals of marketing frauds.

Some investment scams may look like the real deal, but don't fall for them. Gather enough information and facts so you can distinguish the authentic from the fake.

The following are the traditional investment scams out there:

- A deal with a requirement of little or no down payment.
- You are getting your cash back at closing.
- Wholesale deals with obviously inflated prices.

- Mortgage elimination scams.
- Syndication scams (will be discussed in a later chapter).

When faced with people involved in things like this, avoid them like the plague. Don't let them persuade you to invest poorly. Invest wisely and defensively.

10. This is your goal, make it count.

The last principle of defensive investing is to see it as a goal and to make it count. It is no different from seeing a real estate investment as a business and handling it as such. Treat your defensive investments like a goal; hence, make it count in cash and kind.

Define the purpose of your defensive investments, prioritize them in order of importance, analyse your options, and evaluate the outcomes. Know that you are aiming toward sustainable wealth creation; hence it is essential to give it your best.

Defensive investing is the way to succeed in your real estate business. Master the principles and all your dreams shall come true. The next chapter will discuss an important aspect of defensive investing, which is managing your cash flow. Your cash flow is of huge importance in a successful real estate business. Learn how to manage it in the next chapter.

Chapter seven

How to Manage your Cash Flows

In the real estate field, it is essential to have a detailed understanding of what cash flow is all about to enable you to manage it appropriately. Cash flow is the amount of money in circulation to run a particular business. It isn't enough to have just the start-up; it is also essential to have a consistent source of cash to run and flourish the business to your desired level.

Cash reserve is the constant money you have in the bank or at hand that you can spend from on building your business. Unlike cash flow, which is consistent as it comes from the money made from rent, selling of properties, or the extra cash from a mortgage, a cash reserve is a fixed price that keeps reducing as you spend it.

There are so many issues that arise in a real estate business, and as an investor, you must have the necessary resources to salvage the situation. Otherwise, you run into more problems and an ultimate financial disaster. It is essential to have a considerable amount in your cash reserve as a beginner in the real estate business.

The following four factors help to determine the amount to be budgeted into your cash reserve:

- **The rental market:** The lesser the rates of vacancies, the smaller the amount needed in your cash reserve. You will only need a little amount of money to make a vacancy ad in your local newspaper. Also, spend more time screening the tenants, their credit reports, and employment verification to prove that they would be able to pay the rent when due.

- **Cost and time of eviction:** There are times when the expense of evicting a tenant, especially through legal means, may determine the need for a cash reserve. The time frame of evicting a tenant and finding a new tenant may depend on the property, especially a mortgage. A cash reserve must be adequately provided to buffer the effect of that time frame.

- **The property's age:** This will affect your cash reserve as an older property may need repairs, fixing, or renovations - and this may cost a lot. The cost can only be covered by the amount in your cash reserve.

- **The neighbourhood:** Low-income neighbourhoods will lead to a need for more money in the cash reserve, while the opposite is true for high-income neighbourhoods. Neighbourhoods with multi-unit buildings with smaller units will also lessen the amount needed in your cash reserve.

Cash flows and cash reserves are both essential to running a real estate business. When you run out of cash flows, you can rely on your cash reserve to save the day. When you are out of cash reserves, look inward to generate more cash flow.

Cash flows help you make rational business solutions due to the confidence that you have something to rely upon. It helps you to secure deals that need down payments. With enough cash flow and reserves, you can think calmly and make profitable decisions, which is impossible to make when cash-strapped.

You may decide to wait for a higher sales price of property before you start selling; only cash flows and cash reserves can grant you such luxury. It is important to plan for how to generate consistent cash flows and reserves.

Generating cash flows and cash reserves:

- You can create your cash reserves from a good-paying job, long-term investments, or family and friends.
- If you don't have a means for a cash reserve, you can partner with trusted real estate investors to close a deal. Ensure the partner is safe to deal with - no scams involved. Draft a legal document regarding your benefits from such a partnership.

- Save money before investing in significant properties. This can be from your other sources of income or the sales of some belongings.
- Backup funds are essential in generating cash flows and reserves. These backup funds include credit cards and credit lines that can be employed during emergencies.
- Wholesale deals of fix-and-flips to generate cash can also build a cash reserve. If you can't buy the "fixer-upper" properties yourself, you can help the seller find suitable buyers and make money as a middleman. With this, you can employ the double-closing method to buy and flip properties without using your funds. You get to close the second deal from the profit made from the first closing.
- Sometimes your title company may not approve double-closing; an alternative is the contract assignment. The contract assignment is one in which the buyer/seller assigns a purchase contract to another real estate investor to close in their place. Only one closing occurs in a contract assignment - no issues generated.

Cash flows and reserves can be managed by using facts and figures. Invest more to generate more cash flows, make partners secure deals, or source for other means of income. Ensure you spend the money wisely on things that matter and don't overspend. As a beginner in real estate, consult your mentor, browse the internet, or reach out to successful real estate investors to learn more about managing your cash flows effectively.

You must also be vast in closing deals - and you need money to close deals. The next chapter will enlighten you on how to get your closing money. Read and enjoy.

Chapter Eight

Getting 'Closing' Money

Acquiring investments in real estate is very easy with all you have learned from the previous chapters; the critical thing to learn now is how to close deals. Closing off deals requires money the majority of the time. While real estate business requires huge capital and other means of sourcing for funds, the funds needed to close your deals can be outsourced from other methods or gotten through some other transactions. This chapter will enlighten you about the various means of getting the closing money for your real estate business.

These means have been tested and verified to be authentic. If you can still recall my friend Zuri who acquired twelve properties in five years, I am pleased to tell you that Zuri practiced all that was taught in this chapter and was able to source for her closing money with ease. I remember how she kept beaming with smiles after closing her first deal from the money saved up from the rent payments from her townhouse.

There are several means of getting your closing money; study them well and practice whichever suits your situation and financial status.

The following are ways to get your closing money:

Personal savings: If you have up to five figures or more in savings, you can close your deals with your own money. These savings could be from other ventures, a trust fund, or a well-paying job. Personal savings are the best option for cash needed to close deals as there would be no hassle and no need to repay. You can also save up the profit made from the deal for future closings.

Selling off assets: This is another personal means of raising closing money. You may be someone with lots of acquired assets which are no more in use. For instance, cars, boats, expensive furniture, sports gear, and more may be sold at reasonable prices, thus generating the income required to close your deals. If these assets are ones you can't bear to part with, but are not in use, then see it as a temporary parting to gain more in the future.

Cash from your home or rental's equity: Equity from your home is the money earned from renting it out after years of you living there. This was how Zuri started her real estate business. The money earned from a year's rent was used to close her first deal of a rental home. If your home is quite big and you can maximize it as a rental to give you more profits, you can consider downsizing. Moving into a smaller apartment is known as downsizing.

The substantial capital your house is generating can be used to invest in your real estate business. Don't miss out on the opportunity to create more sustainable wealth.

Bring in partners: If you have some cash, but can't meet up with the whole cost needed to close the deal, you can bring in partners. You can leverage on the money from others to close your sales; ensure they are people you trust and have legal backing for all transactions made.

Borrow money from money-lenders and financial institutions: Lending money from private investors and financial institutions can help you source for large amounts of money for large deals. The only issue there is that there are lots of hassles and protocols to deal with. You must also have collateral to borrow colossal amounts of money.

Down payment assistance from governments: There are individual cities and states in the US like Oakland, California, Chicago, Miami, Houston, and so on whose non-profit organizations providing down payments for citizens who haven't owned a home during a certain number of years. For more information, seek information on the state's official website of head office.

There are several other means of getting your closing money which include; credit cards, student loans, borrowing from the real estate commission, selling a part of your property, prepaid rent, tenants' security deposits, lease-options, and so on.

Getting your closing money isn't that hard; through persistence and determination, you can do it. Ensure you don't fall into investment scams and verify your options thoroughly. You can never be too careful, so seek for trusted friends' and allies' opinions and seek consultation from a professional. Beware of predatory lenders.

All of the options above can be employed depending on the type of deal needing to be closed and your financial status. Build wealth to achieve your business goals; closing significant deals will lead you to the financial freedom being propagated by the real estate business.

Now to move forward, we will be discussing how to increase the value of your property. Your property(s) is/are your prized possession(s). You must increase the value(s) of your property(s) to create more sustainable wealth.

You will learn certain things you can do to enhance the value of your property and attract high-income customers. Do read, digest the points, and learn from them.

Chapter Nine

How to Increase the Value of Your Property

Your property tells who you are, and that's why successful real estate investors have high-valued properties. As an aspiring landlord, it is imperative you think from the tenant's point of views as they hold the key to your sustainable wealth.

When you purchase a property for rentals, how to make it attractive for the high-income customers is what runs through your mind as a real estate investor. This implies that the value of your property lies with the type of clients that would make use of the property.

As a beginner in the real estate business, you should know that your clients should be valued to get the maximum profits from your transactions. Whatever conversions you hope to make or type of aspect you want to venture into in real estate, the kind of money you wish to generate all revolve around the CLIENT. Hence, it is crucial you value your esteemed clients to maximise profits.

This chapter is dedicated to teaching you how to increase the value of your property, by valuing your clients, to create sustainable wealth. When you value your customers, it invariably means you will do everything to satisfy their needs. The most important has to do with the property itself.

Like discussed earlier, your property is your prized possession. Hence, you must treat it as such. As a real estate investor, your ultimate goal is to create sustainable wealth; and this can only happen when you have high-valued properties that will attract high-income customers. These high-income clients will generate that sustainable wealth through high-paying and stable rents.

In monetary terms, the value of your property can be estimated as:

Value(V) = Net Operating Income(NOI) ÷ Capitalization rate(R).

For instance, say you have a rental property that brings in a net operating income of $56,000 a year. After various consultations with experts in the real estate business, you figured the property could sell with a capitalisation rate of 8 per cent. With these two values, your property is valued at $700,000.'

$$56000(NOI) \div 0.08(R) = \$700,000(V)$$

If, through some means, you were able to increase the NOI to $65,000, then you would have succeeded in increasing its value by 14 per cent. This means you would have a profit of $112500 as equity.

$$65,000(NOI) \div 0.08(R) = \$812500$$

Let's make it sound even better; you can reduce the risks attached to the property and consequently reduce the cap rate even further to about 7 per cent. With a higher NOI and a lower cap rate, you are bound to have a high-valued property.

$$65,000(NOI) \div 0.07(R) = \$928571(V)$$

From a value of $700,000 to $928571, your property is high-valued. You would probably ask if this is even possible. Yes, it is very possible. As a landlord, with the aim of creating sustainable wealth, you can increase the value of your property by increasing its NOI through high-income customers. The capitalisation price can also be reduced by reducing the risks attached to the properties. All of these would add up to increase your property value.

How can you increase the value of your property? Here's how:

- Put together a new makeover for the interior.
- Ensure safety, security, and convenience at all times.
- Make the rooms the right size according to the function of each.
- Add more storage space.

- Identify what generates noise and try to eradicate or ameliorate it.
- Give your curb the most attractive look ever.
- Engage in services that are beneficial aside from rent collection.
- Make new great conversions from the garage, attic, or basement.
- Convert the property into something more in trend.
- Reduce operating costs to increase your cash flow.
- Old people are important, value them well.
- Improve the overall appearance of your property.
- Adhere to all zoning and building regulations.
- Go with a unique look no client can resist.
- Get rid of disturbances from your neighbours.
- Play a bit of politics.
- Apply market demand to determine rent rates.
- Effective communication with tenants is important.
- Allow your property to stand out amidst competition.
- Create an apartment checklist to ensure you achieve all your goals.

The above and much more are ways to increase the value of the property. You can come up with your own strategy depending on what you desire. Having high-paying clients can be achieved when your property is highly valued.

Chapter Ten

Winning through Negotiations

Finding significant deals is important, but winning them is what matters most. Several factors affect the closing of deals, but few factors make it successful. Negotiation is one of those few factors that can ensure your winning. Negotiating is the act of achieving a purpose through skillful and strategic discussions. Negotiating should be a calm process with no fights or spitting into each other's faces.

Negotiating is an act of discussing to reach an agreement; hence, you have to learn the language to speak, the subtle cues, and the body language involved. Negotiation isn't always a win-win, and as a beginner, the earlier you learn to face reality, the better. Negotiate with buyers, sellers, or clients to earn desired deals. With a more conciliating approach, you can convince anyone to give into what you want.

In the real estate field, many successful investors were able to negotiate their way into their desired deals. It isn't calculus or Greek, but the simple act of convincing the second party to give you what you want.

This chapter will discuss how to win deals through negotiation. It will highlight and explain how to negotiate to gain your desired deals. Winning significant and sizeable deals will help you attain sustainable wealth. Negotiating your way through such deals is essential. So, read on and enjoy.

How to win your deals through negotiating:

1. Know what you want.
This is the first step in the negotiating business. Identify your wants and needs from the deal. Put all of it into consideration while negotiating with the second party. To gain your desired deal, study your strengths and weaknesses in communicating and persuading people to give in. Learn to be charismatic during a negotiating session, dress the part, and sell your strengths.

Knowing yourself will help you negotiate better and secure the deal you are aiming to acquire.

2. Be informed about the property and the neighbourhood.
This is the second step to consider for negotiating that dream deal. As a beginner in the real estate business, it is imperative you have adequate knowledge and information about the property you aim to acquire. This isn't only to enhance negotiations, but to avoid getting into investment

scams. Knowing the neighbourhood is also an additional advantage.

Seek knowledge from the people living in the neighbourhood, the occupants of the property (if any), or the seller himself. With such experience, you have the power to negotiate better and make the most out of it. Do your homework properly to win that deal to desire.

3. Investigate the seller.

This sounds like an FBI mission, but it is crucial in your negotiations. Having vital information about the seller can give you the upper hand at the negotiation table. Run a background check, ask people that are familiar with the seller, ensure you know how they deal. Also seek information about similar deals the seller has carried out to have an insight about the kind of deal you are likely to have.

With this information about the seller, you can know if it's a quick deal or the seller is in search of the highest bidder. You can also ensure the deal is lawful and there are no scams involved. Tilt the deal to your side by having vital information about the seller which is necessary to influence your negotiations.

4. Identify favourable claims.

There are times when the seller brings up claims that are way too exaggerated to support their offer. Such claims include add-ins, appraisals, and a past purchase price that has been exaggerated. It is in your best interest to identify those claims and subtly disprove or undermine them. You can also use the information to your advantage to convince the seller to accept your offer.

It is advisable to use a very subtle approach to avoid causing conflicts or confrontations from the seller. This is the essence of gathering information before going to the negotiating table. Create favourable claims of your own to increase the emotional appeal on your offer.

5. Deal to buy.

What makes some deals last just four or six weeks at most is the buyer's willingness and readiness to buy. Convince the seller that you are ready to buy once you can reach an agreement and a more severe negotiation would be tabled. Coming to the negotiation table prepared to purchase gives you an edge in negotiating your offer.

With all the necessary information about the property and its neighbourhood, the seller, the value, the financial implications, and economic status, you should be prepared to buy when offered a good deal. Explain this to the seller and convince them to accept your offer.

6.   Put in more than you expect in your proposal.

When drafting your offer proposal, put in more than you are expecting. This is because many sellers like to beat down the price until they are assured they have more to gain. With a higher amount than you expect, you can get more, all, or almost all of your offer.

Negotiate based on this amount despite having your real offer in mind. Note that you are aiming to get the most you can from the deal.

7. Your credibility matters.

A good deal requires a lot of credibility on the sides of all parties involved. Negotiate the deal with your credible status. Convince the seller with your character, credit status, capacity, and consistency. With this, you can earn some brownie points from the seller and gain more from your offer. No one likes to deal with someone that is not of credible status.

This means you should portray yourself as a reliable, trustworthy, and competent buyer.

8. Negotiate for yourself.

When it comes to important or huge deals, it is advisable to negotiate them yourself. As a beginner in the real estate business, it is crucial you handle the delivery yourself. This is to ensure that things go well and your interests are adequately considered.

An agent is a no-no, so it's not an option.

9. Never offer the 'split the difference' way out

After a series of negotiations, should you discover that you are at a dead-end, many investors do go for the 'split the difference' way out. It means that the difference between the offers is split up and added to both sides. This means you get lower than you bargained. Even if this is the only way out, never be the first to suggest it.

If the seller suggests it, that's all well and good. You tend to lose more when you do. When the seller initiates it, you can leverage on it to place your offer on the table again and bargain higher.

10. Leave something on the negotiation table to finalise the deal.

Many negotiations do end with one party unhappy with the outcome. You can ensure that you get a lot out of the offer while making the seller feel like they did as well. Leaving a little money out from your proposal, may not be totally beneficial to you, but can earn you a smile from the seller.

Sacrifice a little to maintain cordiality as, who knows, you could need help from the same seller in the future. Don't jeopardise the relationship just because you couldn't compromise a little.

Negotiating is a two-way approach and you must tread with caution so as not to cause conflicts. Have access to all necessary information to enable you to get the most from the deal. Utilise a subtle approach to disprove or undermine claims from the seller. Above all, with adequate negotiation, you can win your huge deals and generate sustainable wealth.

Chapter Eleven

How to Invest for Maximum Gain

Real estate investment has been proven to be an authentic investment that can guarantee sustainable wealth. You have learned how real estate can serve as a pathway to sustainable wealth. You also discovered the numerous ways to build wealth and how to raise money in real estate. How to handle your real estate investments as a business and the principles of defensive investing have been discussed, and you learned a lot as well.

Achieving sustainable wealth through real estate is all about making money and maximising your gains. This chapter focuses on how to invest for maximum gain. There are several branches of real estates to venture into, and each can bring you sustainable wealth. These aspects of real estate can be explored to maximise your gain. Read this chapter and learn more.

Investing for maximum gain focuses on how to expand your host of money-making ventures in real estate business. It involves discovering the several ways of making more money in your estate business.

As earlier discussed, the business of real estate is beyond buying and selling. As a beginner in the real estate business, you must know the other means of investing in real estate to maximise your gain. This way, you have multiple income streams, and you get to achieve the desired real estate goals.

The following are the means of investing to maximise your gains:

1. Long-term residential rentals:

This is one of the traditional methods of investing in real estate business. Long-term residential rentals refer to the process of owning a rental property and renting it out to tenants. This is a great investment plan as it is consistent and stable. It helps to generate adequate cash flows needed to run your real estate business.

It is an undeniable fact that the population increases and there is always a demand for residences to accommodate the growth. This leads to people renting homes, or buying for those fortunate enough. There are always young adults who want to live alone and college students who want out of college dorms or on-campus residences.

People migrate from one town to another and need a place to stay either temporarily or permanently. All these put together implies that residential rentals are in high demand and a lucrative way of investing to maximise profits.

To make this investment worthwhile, ensure you own a great place that is attractive to your desired customers. Also, ensure it is in a great location to serve as an advantage. Ensure your tenancy contracts are beneficial for your desired clients.

Long-term residential rentals, if properly managed, can result in retirement investments. It can also be passed down from generation to generation - hence, serving as long-lasting wealth for your family.

2. Real estate ETFs and mutual funds:

A real estate exchange-traded fund (ETF), is a collection of stocks or bonds in a single fund. These funds are similar to index funds and mutual funds, due to the fact that they come with the same broad diversification and low costs overall.

These stocks come from real estate investments trusts (REITs) and are authentic. To maximise your gain, you can invest in this area with the profits you have made in order to earn more. It is safe once you get the hang of it.

Real estate mutual funds are another means of maximising profit and generating sustainable wealth. These funds have low costs and low track record, hence, can serve as a side attraction in optimising your gain.

3. Fix-and-flip investments:

This is another traditional means of real estate investment. This investment is very profitable as it allows you to maximise profit with small investments. Conversions of properties according to market trends and demands can also be looked into. It differs from residential rentals as these homes have to be converted from their original forms to something more enticing.

Learn the act of renovating homes with a low budget. You should use the principle of majoring on the inexpensive repairs and minoring on the expensive ones, for starters. Learn creative ways of doing renovations without much money. Consult experts in this field and make your investments count.

Fix-and-flip type of real estate investment is an advisable real estate investment for beginners in the real estate business. Ensure you verify the property you want to flip properly to avoid investment scams. Being creative is all it takes to make it big in this type of investment.

4. Short sales:

There are times that a real estate investor may be behind in the payment on their mortgage and need a way out. If the property is yet to be foreclosed, then a short sale may occur. All the parties involved in the mortgage possession must reach an agreement before such transactions occur. After the deal, the property is sold for a lesser price than what is left of the mortgage. This is a great chance to invest and buy below the market value.

This investment is lucrative, but also risky. You have to pay in cash, and it may not be safe to do so. It is, however, profitable as you get to inspect the property and know what you are getting into. Do a fair job of negotiating, and you could be leaving with an investment worth hundreds to thousands more than you invested.

With adequate patience and an eye for a good investment, you can pull it off and maximise your gain.

5. Real estate Investment Trusts (REITs):

For investments in real estate without owning physical property, real estate investment trusts are the key. They allow you to invest in properties without owning them physically. This aspect of real estate is new and has been discovered to be profitable for those that know how it works.

With REITs, you can achieve your real estate goals through diversifying. It is a long term investment - and as long as you know the market trends, you will be fine. Invest your profits in this and maximise your gains. Attain everlasting wealth with real estate investments trusts.

6. Vacation rentals:

Think about this - the massive influx of tourists in Miami, Los Angeles, and California translates into more wealth for you. Having vacation homes in places with tourist attractions can be a good strategy in maximising your gain. You can buy reasonable properties and turn them into vacation homes for tourists.

You can make a lot from this type of investment and save up a lot. It has been proven to be highly profitable and secure as an investment in real estate. Managing a vacation home isn't expensive. Hence, there are more ways to make money. List your property on the internet and create a website to attract more customers.

Another interesting fact about this type of investment is that you may not even own a single property to participate in it. All you need do is to set up connections and manage vacation homes to maximise your gain. Utilise the power of leverage to create profitable relationships to give you an edge. Come up with great strategies that would attract clients to the vacation homes you want to manage. Manage them well and earn great reviews for the promotion of your business.

7. Hard-money lending / private investing:

Hard money lending is short-term lending of loans to people without financial means to close their deals or invest in real estate. This method of investing is fast and has a huge interest rate. Many people are in desperate need of money to close significant and profitable deals. Identify such real estate investors and sweep in to save the day.

As a private investor, you are assured of getting your money back when due. Since your interest rate is also high, you get to generate a lot of income. To kick-start this business, ensure you have a significant amount of capital or partner with other reliable investors for this. You don't need huge money, just enough to start and you can keep refinancing with the profits made.

It will increase your cash flow and give you opportunities to save enough to invest in great deals as well. This is an authentic way of achieving sustainable wealth in the real estate business.

8. Commercial real estate

As a beginner in the real estate business, it is advisable to focus on a type of investment. As time goes on and you make progress, you can diversify and start looking into other income streams. Commercial real estate is the owning and managing of multiple units of properties ranging from residential homes to office buildings, to shopping malls, and so on. Diversification will boost your cash flows and help you attain sustainable wealth faster.

Many successful real estate investors today are into commercial real estate. It is profitable and long-term. It is the type of investment to pass from one generation to another. It is a great way to maximise your gain in real estate.

The above real estate investments are ways to maximise your gain in the real estate business. With the goal of everlasting wealth in real estate, you can't afford to put all your eggs in one basket. Spread your wings to generate more wealth and be successful in your real estate business. As a beginner, it won't be easy; but with hard work, persistence, and patience you will get there. If Zuri can own 12 properties in five years, nothing should stop you from achieving the same and much more.

All you need is to be visionary, ambitious, and ready to take action at all times. Your reading this book is a sign that you desire sustainable wealth and are a step closer to achieving it.

Chapter Twelve

Becoming a Successful Landlord

Congratulations in advance on owning your first rental property. Yes, you deserve the congratulations for becoming a potential landlord. If you understand everything that has been discussed in this book up to this point, then you deserve the compliment. You can proudly call yourself a real estate investor; all you need to do is to take actions.

Have you ever wondered how you will feel when you become a successful landlord? If you haven't, then start thinking about it. Owning a property is cool; and renting the property out and making cool cash from it is a step toward your real estate dreams. When you become a successful landlord, then you can say you have achieved your goals.

This chapter will focus on grooming you to become a successful landlord. You have learned how to increase the value of your property to attract high-income clients in a previous chapter. You will learn how to get those clients, how to make their stay memorable, and how to keep them. So, pick up your pen and learn more.

If all you dream of is becoming a successful landlord, then listen up, YOU CAN DO IT. The whole journey to get there may seem long and complicated; but really, after reading this book up to this point, you are halfway there. All you need is to put it all into actions and make your dreams come true.

Having a rental property and maintaining it with tenants is not an easy task. As a beginner in the real estate business, you have to decide if you want to call the shots yourself or recruit someone capable of doing that. Property management can be quite taxing and demanding; and it's not necessary you take on the role yourself.

Property management may be through hired management or self-management. Hired management leads to passive control of your property by delegating managerial activities to a caretaker or a property management company. This process allows you to have more time on your hands to do other activities, as well as providing professional management of your property.

A caretaker is someone hired with the knowledge and experience of property management. The caretaker looks into all the necessary details of property management you delegate. You may decide to give them almost full autonomy in handling your tenants and the property. You may also be involved in important decision making, policies, procedures, and all other significant issues concerning your property and tenants.

It is advisable to employ an older and more experienced person as a beginner, to reach a level of professionalism and avoid your property being managed by unfit hands. You may also give the job to a reliable tenant, whom you are giving all or almost all rent off as incentive. Whichever options you chose, ensure you recruit a trustworthy and competent person.

A property management company is one that specialises in managing multiple rental units of different property owners. This company is experienced and has competent professionals skilled in property management. It may be expensive and not specific in strategies, but when it comes to professionalism, it's the right choice.

Self-management is the act of managing your property by yourself. As a beginner in the real estate business, it is advisable you go into this, at least for your first property, and subsequently you can employ hired management. You may ask how it's possible with no experience or knowledge whatsoever. Here's the reply; it's possible, for you have this book to guide you right!

Self-management helps to save costs of hiring someone or a company. With self-management, you can learn first-hand the process of managing a property. You also get to be exposed to the world of property management and learn the ropes of how the market works. You are allowed to make mistakes, take risks, and move ahead, sure you are doing it right. Exercise patience, consult with other experienced real estate investors in this field, and read to learn more about it.

For adequate and excellent self-management, you must learn how to become a successful landlord. You will learn the ten principles of becoming a successful landlord.

1. Understand the buyer's risks.

It is an indisputable fact that buying a property comes with lots of risks. As a beginner, you have to ensure you avoid them by understanding what those risks are. When purchasing a property, be sure it is the one you truly want and you have the necessary means to acquire it. Inspect the property correctly and ask for a formal report on the status of the property. Consult a professional in property inspection to get your desired results.

Do a background check on the property by asking neighbours, occupants, and others that know about it. Ask them how the property has been run in the past, how they perceive it, its advantages and disadvantages. Ask if there had been any issues, civil or criminal, attached to the property. Ask all the right questions to avoid falling into investments scams.

If the property is currently occupied by tenants, ask for tenant rent tolls and files. This will enable you to have an insight into the tenants occupying the property and their rent payment attitudes. Verify security deposits transferred from the seller to you. Confirm that it is authentic and have documentation to that effect.

Learn about the rules and laws binding the property in that area or vicinity. Ask for any permits, licenses, zoning, building regulations, and occupancy laws associated with the property. Ask carefully and ensure they are rules you can abide by.

Get copies of warranties and service contracts the tenants signed with the seller. Review them properly and ensure you are okay with them and can maintain them all. After purchasing the property, arrange for insurance coverage to minimise future losses. With all these things taken into consideration, you can be assured you are acquiring a property with little or no risks.

2. Have the property suitable for rentals.

If your rental property still has tenants from the previous owner, do well to honour the existing rental agreements. Comply with the rules and regulations and start looking into vacancies as soon as various tenants' contracts are coming to an end.

To prepare for vacancies, you have to think about the group of tenants you would like to accommodate. Your goal is sustainable wealth through real estate investment, so ensure that you target high-income clients or high-paying clients. Clients like college students, Senior families, young professionals, empty nesters, and so on are examples of high-paying clients.

To begin the process of making your property suitable for renting and to attract high-paying clients, clean and paint to give it a new look. Do thorough inspections to ensure every appliance is working. All broken locks, windows, doors and screens should be repaired or replaced. Make renovations if possible and install new fittings to make it suitable and attractive for renting.

It's not enough to have the place good-looking and attractive; adding value through tenant-friendly services is the total package. As the landlord, ensure you are friendly and approachable to create a good rapport with your tenants. Allow for some freedom and tenant autonomy by accepting pets, furniture and appliances.

Put in hot-button features to attract your desired clients. Hot-button features like great kitchens and bathrooms, amazing views, vast storage, nice parking lots, study areas, soundproof walls, open floor plans, and roommate-friendly plans can be included in your preparation.

Create friendly terms and conditions, and make security deposits and rent payments flexible by allowing for payments in instalments. Include tenant likes and dislikes when deciding on the rental rates. In essence, ensure your tenants are comfortable leaving and happy with the lease rules and regulations, terms and conditions, and physical features.

3. Attract high-paying residents.

To attract high-paying residents, you have to put up your vacancies in places with potential high-paying clients. Utilise the media and promote your vacancy ads to attract your desired customers. Put up ads in commercial areas, on campuses, and other places where your potential clients can be found. Put together a sales message that highlights the hot-button features of your property as well as benefits for the residents. Explain why your property is the best, and it should be chosen by your desired customers.

When potential clients show interest in your property, ensure you screen them all thoroughly. Ask for credit scores and records, employment verification (current and past employment), rental history, and photo identification to verify they are fit to be your tenants. Ask the chosen tenants to pay their rent and security deposits before moving into your property. Don't listen to flimsy stories, so you don't fall victim of investments scams.

Learn all housing and occupancy rules and adhere to the reasonable ones. Create a waiting list, so as not to lose out on other potential clients while screening some.

4. Promote a stress-free move-in.

As a landlord, it is essential you have move-in policies and procedures. These policies and procedures should centre on creating an excellent landlord-tenant relationship, rules and regulations of occupancy, and the condition of the property ready for move-in.

To create a long-lasting landlord-tenant relationship, ensure you are observant and always ready to attend to the needs of your tenants. Make friendly occupancy terms and conditions, and be prepared to attend to all matters affecting your tenants as regards your property. Create rules that will put your property in good use by the tenants, as well as allow the tenants to enjoy their stays. Be flexible with your standards, but ensure you enforce the rules and regulations strictly and fairly.

Prepare the property and have it ready for move-in. Don't leave any room for complaints from your tenants on the first day. Be prepared to impress your tenants and make their stay memorable.

5. Retain high-income residents.

It is one thing to attract your desired clients; it is another to retain them. As a landlord, you must be on your toes at all times to ensure you don't lose your high-income customers. This can be achieved by paying attention to details and attending to matters promptly. Don't allow your tenants to have a heap of complaints for you at all times.

Keep your tenants informed at all times. When there is any new development regarding the occupancy, ensure you notify your tenants promptly. Don't wait until the last minute; act fast and do things proactively.

It's not all the time that things run smoothly; the stairs may break one day, the door locks may break, or the ceilings may creak. It is your duty as the landlord to prevent all of these things from happening in due time through preventive maintenance. Don't wait until it happens; periodic checks can serve as an eye-opener to potential damage. Fix them when discovered to avoid the next occurrence.

There are times that despite all preventive maintenance, things get faulty. This is due to wear and tear; as a landlord, ensure you have a contingency plan for when this occurs. Have the best handymen and service companies ready to cater for such occurrences. Don't inconvenient your tenants; respond well and put things back in order.

6.   Increase your rent, only and only if it is favourable.

To create sustainable wealth through real estate investments, you need to increase your cash flows from time to time and generate more profits. Increasing rent is one way to go about it. The problem here is, an increase in rent can lead to the risk of losing a good tenant. It goes without saying that, in as much as you want to generate more income, only increase the rent when it is favourable.

There are specific market periods that support an increase in rent. When rentals are in high demands and market competition has reduced, an increase in rent is favourable. Study the trends and know when to propose and implement a rent increase. Verify the market support before offering a rent increase to avoid losing your clients.

Communicate and present facts to your tenants to support your proposal. You can show your tenants property taxes, property insurance, and maintenance expenses to back your claims. This allows your tenants to reason along with you and invariably agree with you.

Give incentives as a way of appreciating the agreement to the increase. You can install new security systems, add new appliances, and do some refurbishing. Ensure the increase is gradual and frequent to allow the tenants to pay without trouble. A significant increment at once may lead to complaints and an ultimate loss of tenants.

7. Expect and handle special problems.

It's not all the time that things are smooth and rosy. Your tenants may suddenly face certain setbacks like divorce, accidents, ill health, unemployment, or bankruptcy, amongst others. It is important you show empathy and understanding to your tenants' plights at this point.

It is a good thing to show understanding, but remember, this is a business and it must be handled as such. Ensure that the rents are still paid despite all. You can suggest help from social workers, charities, or other means of financial support. If it is too difficult for your distressed tenants, negotiate a voluntary move-out.

If it comes to the point of eviction, do it the right way - that is, legally. Do it from a legal standpoint; put together a written notice of the legitimate action taken. There must be time to cure the breach of contract and time to prepare for a hearing. Allow the tenants to have defences to be fair in your dealings. There must be a notice of days the tenants have to move out before being forcefully evicted.

8. Maintain your property.
In becoming a successful landlord, it is crucial you manage your property to avoid wear and tear, complaints from your tenants, or the ultimate loss of tenants.

Maintenance is vital in the rental business. This minimises complaints from your tenants and attracts potential residents. Enhance the value of your property through maintenance. There are different forms of maintenance that can be carried out in property management.

- **Preventive and Corrective Maintenance:** This involves the repairs and replacements of faulty appliances or parts of the property. It also comprises fixing of places with the potential of getting faulty in due time. Doors, windows, electrical appliances, floors, are in this category.

- **Custodial Maintenance:** This form of maintenance focuses on keeping the property neat and tidy. It involves hiring a waste collection service, a cleaning service, and so on.

- **Cosmetic Maintenance:** This is the maintenance of the property's looks. The floors and grounds are inspected, peeling walls are repainted, carpet stains are removed or carpets are replaced, burnt countertops are replaced

- **Safety and Security Maintenance:** This maintenance is aimed at improving the safety and security of your tenants. Repair broken stairs, lightning, doors, windows, or latches. Ensure security systems like smoke alarms are intact. For potential threats to safety and security, ask tenants to contact you and respond appropriately.

9. Plan for a smooth Move-out.

There is no lifetime rental agreement, so it is expected that your tenants' contracts come to an end. To ensure this process is smooth and without hassle, ask for a written notice at least thirty days or more before the due date.

A damage inspection should be carried out a few days before or on the day of the move-out. Ask for damage claims if there are damages caused by the tenants. Ensure you are professional and maintain a good relationship with your tenants until the very end.

After the move-out, start preparing for vacancies and accommodation of new tenants.

10. Increase your cash flows.

As discussed earlier, in chapter seven, there are several ways of managing and increasing your cash flows. Ensure you implement those methods to increase the cash flows needed to maintain your property and make more profits. You can also invest in refinancing with your current cash flows to gain more and achieve sustainable wealth.

Becoming a successful landlord isn't a "day job" as it requires many efforts, dedication, proper planning, and patience. Learn the ropes of becoming a successful landlord and apply what you know. You are assured of achieving your dreams of sustainable wealth in the real estate business.

Chapter Thirteen

Exit Strategies: Have Varying Options

There are many people out there testing the waters of real estate investment without knowing the rudiments. Little wonder, they have experienced many failed investment deals. Successful real estate investors are knowledgeable and informed about investment deals and options to exit. This has helped them achieve sustainable wealth in the real estate business. As a beginner in the real estate business, you should learn about having several exit strategies before you begin investing.

This chapter will enlighten you on the several options under "Exit Strategies" you can choose from when investing. It also focuses on the factors that determine your choice of an exit strategy and factors that can allow the exit strategy not to go as planned. Get your pen and book and learn the secrets of exit strategies.

What Is a Real Estate Exit Strategy?

From the name, it can be implied that a real estate exit strategy is a plan in which the real estate investor intends to remove him/herself from a real estate investing deal. An exit strategy is a proposed plan of what the real estate investor will do with the investment property.

There are several exit strategies that you as a real estate investor can employ when investing in a deal. You can either have the exit strategy as an original investment plan or decide on it as things unfold during the process of investing. The best method is to have an exit strategy along with your investment plan.

So many real estate investors have failed to identify the importance of exit strategies, which is evident in their investment plans with no exit options.

Why is Real Estate Exit Strategy Important?

Establishing an appropriate real estate exit strategy will not only provide you as a real estate investor with a plan of action, but it will also minimise risks. As a real estate investor, you can evaluate potential exit strategies before purchasing investment properties; this will expose you to the risks associated with the investment and help you avoid them.

Having a specific exit strategy is vital to the success of your investment, as the right exit option will result in maximised profits and sustainable wealth. It's always safer to enter a real estate investment deal with a clear picture of the profit you can get from the real estate property when exiting from the investing deal. This implies that having a financial goal and an exit strategy can save you a spot of money and generate long-lasting wealth in your real estate business.

In cases of unexpected emergencies, a real estate exit strategy can serve as a way out of that emergency. You may be in dire need of cash; with a real estate exit strategy you can sell the property faster and cash out.

As a real estate investor, you should be looking into expanding your investment coast and building your investment portfolio. With an exit strategy, you get to learn how to manage these different investment belongings. You will also know how to react and the way forward when an investment isn't giving you your desired outcome.

To reduce the potential risks and increase the profits in your real estate investments, you must understand the essence of having an exit option. In generating sustainable wealth through real estate business, you must identify, understand and implement the various real estate exit strategies available.

Various Real Estate Exit Strategy Available

Having the right ideology about exit strategies will go a long way in achieving your dreams of sustainable wealth.

1. Fix-and-Flip

This real estate exit strategy is a typical profit-generating plan, as it allows you as a real estate investor to sell the real estate property at full market value. It involves purchasing investment properties at low market value, putting them under repair, renovating them, and then selling them for more than the original investment costs - that is, the purchase price plus repair costs.

As a real estate investor willing and seeking to execute this exit strategy option, you must be aware of market trends and demands. You must also have the capacity to increase the value of your real estate investment properties.

2. Buy-and-Hold

This exit strategy is ideal if, as a real estate investor, you are looking to build up equity in a real estate property. It has a similar option to that of fix-and-flip. The difference here is that instead of selling the renovated property, as a real estate investor, you can choose to hold it for some time and rent it out to generate cash flow for your real estate business.

As appreciation and equity increase the value of the property, it can be put on the market to be sold for a profit. You must also know market trends here to achieve your purpose.

3. Wholesaling

In this type of exit strategy, as a real estate investor, you act as the middleman between a property seller and a property buyer. Basically, as a real estate wholesaler, you will scout for cheap property from distressed buyers and quickly sell for a profit margin. After the purchase, you then place the investment property under a purchase contract and then sell this contract to the buyer for a small profit.

This exit strategy is implemented in investments wherein you need to end the deal because it saves you time.

4. Seller Financing

This exit strategy is employed when exiting an investment deal which continues to produce a profit. In this investment plan, the seller finances the real estate investing deal and acts as a bank. Then, there is an exchange of promissory note indicating an interest rate and a repayment schedule between the buyer and the seller.

This exit strategy is beneficial to real estate sellers as they are awarded monthly payments to cover the mortgage loan. They also get to have a nice increased return on the investments due to interest.

5. Rent to Own (Lease Option)

In this type of exit strategy, you are allowed to rent your property to a tenant, with the option to purchase it after a set period. You may save a part of the monthly payments towards the purchase of the property.

The above types of exit strategies can be employed in any investment deal as desired.

Factors Influencing the Choice of an Exit Strategy

You can decide on whatever exit strategy you want for a specific investment. However, certain factors will affect your decision. These factors will help you determine the suitable exit strategy for a particular investment deal. They are:

- Short-term and long-term goals
- Experience in real estate
- Closing time
- Sale price
- Value of the property
- Terms and condition of the property
- Market trends
- Market demands
- Available financing options
- The profit potential of the investment
- Location of the property

Understanding these factors will allow a real estate investor to determine which of the real estate exit strategies they should follow.

Factors That Can Demerit an Exit Strategy

As a real estate investor, you should know that an exit strategy may not go as planned due to certain factors. These factors are:

- Depreciation
- Loss of rent as a result of tenancy issues

- Unforeseen maintenance expenses, which may cancel out profits
- Decreased value of the property as a result of poor property management
- When a property cannot be flipped as a result of no demand, failed escrow, or backing out of the partnership by a partner

Having more than one exit strategy is the key to solving the above issue. As a beginner in the real estate business, it is best to know when to opt out of an investment deal, when it is profitable to sell, and why it is important to have several exit strategies at your disposal.

Chapter Fourteen

How to Prevent Investment Scams

Real estate is not an easy business; finding the right property, organising the proper funding, and managing a rental take a lot of time and effort. And just like in any business, there are people who want to scam you out of your hard work.

This chapter focuses on real estate investment scams - the various types, how to identify them, what to do when you do, and how to prevent yourself from falling for those scams.

The art of scamming has evolved over time, and the more types of investment, the bigger and broader the scam. Con artists are becoming more sophisticated in their scamming methods, thus increasing their detriments. No one is immune to investment scams, but you can be careful enough to avoid falling for them.

What are real estate investment scams?

Scams are fraudulent activities carried out with the ultimate goal of deception for an ulterior motive.

There are certain people who derive pleasure in allowing others to work for money and deceiving them to get away with that money. For real estate, investment scams are aimed at duping real estate investors, buyers, and sellers into investment deals that are detrimental to them.

Real estate investment scams have been in existence since just about the time real estate investments were discovered. Scammers in the real estate field mostly target beginners and not-so-experienced investors. It is undeniable that what you don't know, you can't question. This principle is what real estate investment scammers employ in carrying out their evil plans.

Real estate investment scams involve a fraud proposing investment deals that are fake, detrimental and aimed to make you lose your wealth. Promises are made but not kept, what is being paid for isn't done or carried out, fake qualifications, disappearing after collecting rents, and security deposits of property not owned, are all characteristics portrayed by real estate investment frauds.

As a beginner in real estate business, you have to be vigilant and observant, know the signs, and watch out for them. There are remedies for real estate investment scams. Criminal prosecution, rescission of contracts, punitive damages, and internal revenue service penalties are examples of such remedies.

To have a better understanding of real estate investment scams, you must know the various types of investment frauds available.

Types of Real Estate Scams

1. Loan Modification Scams:

This real estate investment scam is a notorious one, as it preys on many investors, especially beginners. It is something that a real estate investor like you should be wary of. The typical victims of this scam are homeowners who are struggling to pay a mortgage or are facing foreclosure. A scammer will act as a 'lender' and will offer to 'modify' the loan so that the owner pays lesser amounts. They may even assure a 'guarantee' of protection from foreclosure. But of course, the owner has to pay a fee, usually an upfront fee - a fraud alert. The investor will also be asked to send personal information, including a bank account number, to the scammer.

These scammers are incredibly cunning. Some scammers will have a website with a government logo or even that end in ".gov". However, they are avoidable. Do not get involved with third parties when it comes to a mortgage. Deal with your mortgage company and them only, even when facing difficulty in paying.

The fraud alerts of loan modifications are demanding upfront payments and asking for personal information. It is illegal for a company to ask for upfront payments; make sure you know that! Also, beware of anyone or any agency asking for your bank account information. Chances are, they want to scam you!

2. Rental Scams:

Investors interested in buying a rental will first turn to the internet for their property search. This is just pure fact, and the actual number of investors who turn to the internet is over 90%. Equipped with this knowledge, scam artists turn to the Internet as well. What they then do is select an actual listing, that is not theirs, and post it on their website - or even on commonly used sites like Craigslist. The craftier computer scammers may even hack the site of the original listing and replace the written information with some of their own. The investor is then asked to wire the payment to a third party.

These real estate investment scammers do not necessarily need the Internet. The more old-fashioned con artists will offer property at a very low price. During an open house, they will ask interested buyers to fill out an application and pay some fees. Then, if they contact you or you contact them, they will tell you that your application has been rejected.

Whether the scammer is online or not, an investor will be asked to wire the payment, no matter the kind of payment. The scammer will demand payment, even if you two have not met yet or signed any legal documents. These investors will also claim they are out of the country - another warning to be aware of.

All of these are big no-no's you should watch out for. To learn how to report rental scams officially, read this.

3. Mortgage Syndication Scams:

A mortgage is said to be in syndication when there is a marriage of equals, people with money to spare, and people with a solid, vetted business plan/venture. Every party is aware of such marriage risks and can function due to the diligence required to ascertain their level of risk.

All the mortgage syndication frauds involve the cloaking of asymmetry or risk in an unequal relationship. This means one of the parties has a lot more information than the other. One of the parties will generally know more about the business than the other. One party will be more educated than the other. One party will have more access to professionals than the other.

In most cases, the mortgage syndication company will be offering an investor that has never had any additional information or exposure to the investment, a higher level.

4. Seminar Scams:

The one thing all real estate investment scams have in common, aside from scamming investors, is that they put on the pretence of wanting to help an investor and end up duping them. As a beginner in the real estate business, you are susceptible to such pretence, because of the eagerness to break even. In seminar scams, the scammer might provide actual help as a form of bait in achieving their aim.

Just like loan modification scams, seminar scams soared during the housing bubble. This scam is primarily a workshop by an 'expert'. The expert will provide gullible investors with "get-rich-quick" tips, some of them being actually valuable and factual. This unconsciously plants seeds of trust the investor has for the expert. Then, the scammer will offer investors a property that is available "for a limited time" or additional classes that cost thousands of dollars.

If investors buy one of the limited properties hastily, they may not be able to review the property as accurately as they usually would. Then, only after the purchase, the investor realises that the property may be flawed in some ways and has taken part in a bad investment.

Falling for the second trap is just as detrimental to the investor. The course turns out to offer investors with basic and repetitive information. This leaves them feeling frustrated since they spent thousands of dollars on a course that provided so little.

Once an investor becomes entangled in one of these real estate investment scams, it can become difficult to get out of. Why? Well, by signing an agreement document with the scammer, the investor is limited with legal action against the scammer.

To avoid these real estate investment scams, do your research. Research the 'expert', the property, and courses they may present. The research will also help you find certified and trustworthy experts and any companies they are affiliated with.

5. Title Scams:

Last on the list of most common real estate investment scams, is title fraud. It is the least common of the ones mentioned on the list, but it can be just as or more destructive. This scam could potentially result in identity theft.

This is how it works - a scammer will use false documents to pose as a home seller. The scammer will recommend to buyers not to purchase title insurance. This leaves the buyer with a detrimental investment. The scammer may also request personal information from the buyer in order to sell.

Title scams can be avoided through the purchase of title insurance. This helps to protect the buyer from the false impersonation of the seller. The title insurance company will verify the deal and search for any mortgage attached to the property.

The above real estate investment scams are quite common, among others. These investment frauds are common and similar to the real deal, hence, can be mistaken for an authentic deal. Learn to distinguish them properly and be prepared to avoid them

How to Identify Real Estate Investment Scams

There are many real estate investors out there. Some are testing out their luck in the business of real estate, some have purposes they want to achieve with it, and some others are out there to reap the benefit of others' efforts. To avoid being a victim of real estate investment scams, you must be able to identify them when you see them. This way, you can run away from them as far as possible.

Many investment frauds try to mimic the real deal so you don't suspect them. However, since it isn't the authentic deal, certain phrases or clauses stand out, hence pointing them out as scams. Some investment scams are too similar to real investment deals, and this may cause you to miss out on real and significant deals. With proper research and knowing how not to fall for investment scams, you can make it out unscathed.

Phrases and clauses that can be identified in common investment deals:

- 'No money down' mortgage deals
- Deals with unrealistic guarantees
- Deals that sell the dream, rather than sharing the knowledge
- Deals that negotiate by creating a sense of scarcity
- 'Risk-free'
- 'Magic'
- 'Secrets'
- 'Bullet-proof'

- 'Get rich quick'
- 'Bearers bonds'
- 'Advance fee' on mortgage loans
- 'Judgement-proof'
- 'Nevada Corporations' outside Nevada, among others.

With the above phrases and clauses, you can spot an investment fraud easily and prevent yourself from falling for them.

How to Avoid Falling for Investment Scams

Ensure that you know what investment scams are and that you can identify them and the various types available. It is crucial you learn how to prevent yourself from falling for investment frauds. This way, you don't get to see that ugly aspect of real estate business.

Rules and regulations regarding investment scams differ from state to state. Having the right information is vital and acting on it is the best solution. When you are faced with an investment scam, these are the things to do:

1. Research and gather the correct information.

Knowledge is power only when it's at your fingertips. We are in the jet age, where things have been made easy. As a real estate investor, you must be a researcher and have the ability to gather information before investing. This is to your advantage as you will have an eye opener into what you are getting involved in.

Before investing in any real estate deal, be sure to do proper research. Know all the information about it. Know why the seller wants to sell and at what price. Know the market value of a property and the potential profits that can be generated from it, before you secure such deals.

2. Check for certifications, licensure and all other types of credentials.

Phony investors portray themselves as the real deal, only they don't have the necessary credentials to back their claims. As a real estate investor, don't start negotiating a deal until you have verified some of the necessary credentials involved. This will serve as a guarantee that you are on the right track. Check out all property certificates and licensure as well as those of the investor, buyer, or seller.

Know the credit score and records of your potential tenants before leasing out your property. When you want to hire a caretaker or a property management company, check out their reviews from previous clients and ask for certifications and licenses.

3. Consult professionals on all issues.

One mistake that too many beginners like you in the real estate business make is having an 'I-Know-What-I-am-doing' mentality. Since you are new, not experienced, and trying to find your feet, it is in your best interest to have successful and experienced real estate investors as mentors or allies. When you have such persons as mentors or allies, you are sure to have a good backing.

Consult these professionals on issues related to real estate investments. There are also professionals like real estate attorneys and tax advisors that you should consult when the need arises. Don't live in your shell, believing you can achieve it on your own, until you fall victim of investment frauds. Rather, ask questions of the right people.

4. Be objective and rational.

One of the crucial qualities a real estate investor must possess is being clearheaded. This quality is vital in investing in the real estate business. Being objective in your dealings will allow you avoid some investment scams. With objectivity, you can think from a neutral point of view, weighing all options. You also make decisions based on facts and figures and not mere hearsay.

Being rational will enable you to avoid giving in to emotional sways from investment frauds. You must be level-headed and composed. Hold conversations with confidence and don't be moved by unnecessary and false claims.

5. Don't be in haste.

Real estate is a long-term investment; hence, there is plenty of time to secure a great deal, purchase property, rent it out to your desired customers, or sell when it is profitable. Though some deals are time-bound, there is still no need to be in a rush. It is safe for you to take your time to gather knowledge and experience before investing in some deals.

There are many real estate investment traps out there, and by taking your time, you can avoid them. Dig into everything surrounding the deal and if you are faced with potential scams, abandon such deal. Take your time to investigate the seller, buyer, or lender.

6. Make it official.

Nothing is official until you put your signature on it. A deal isn't secured yet until you have documents in your name bearing your signature. Don't trust the words of people; rather allow them to put their words into writing and have it bound by the law.

Don't let yourself be swayed by sweet talkers that a legal document isn't needed. Ensure it is provided; otherwise, let go of such deals.

7. Do your homework yourself.

Regardless of what the deal is, as a real estate investor, it is advisable you do the work yourself. Delegating it may backfire. Check out properties yourself; visit the location and the local government yourself; cross-check what was written in the contract to what you can see.

As a beginner in the real estate business, it is essential you do all of this yourself. You are the only ONE that can have the best interest of your investment at heart, don't let others jeopardise it.

8. Ask questions and satisfy your curiosity.

Finally, when any question comes to your mind about the property or deal, ask. Ensure that you know everything about what you plan to get involved with, whether it's a property, deal, data, or anything else. Pique your interest and satisfy your curiosity.

There are also times you need to trust your gut instincts. This should be done after you have satisfied your curiosity. With all questions asked, you can be assured of what you are doing.

Real estate investment scams are real and it would be devastating to fall victim. This goes without saying that, you have to be careful and ensure you don't fall into such traps.

Chapter Fifteen

You've Got It, Now KEEP It

Finally, it's the last chapter in this book about creating sustainable wealth through real estate. If you have read the whole book to this point, you deserve a round of applause. The journey of a thousand miles begins with just one step. You have embarked on the journey of long-lasting wealth through real estate and reading this book is a huge step to reach your destination.

You have learned a lot about the real estate business and how you can generate sustainable wealth through it. You know the practical guides, tips, and principles needed to aide you in reaching your dreams. You have been exposed to how to maximise your gain, explore various exit strategies, and avoid investment scams. Now is the time to learn how to keep your real estate investments, so you don't end up losing all you have gained.

This chapter focuses on the things to do to protect your property and investments. It also serves as a guide on how to avoid liabilities or legal issues surrounding the real estate business. All in all, you are going to learn how to treasure your investments. Do read and enjoy!

Real estate investments may be long-term, but if not properly managed or maintained, there may have short-term challenges. It is in your best interest as a real estate investor that you take proper care to ensure you don't lose your hard work, diligence, persistence, and patience in one swoop. As a beginner in the real estate business, having learned a lot up to this point, you've got it, now KEEP it!

The following are ways to keep your real estate investments:

1. Make your tenants your priority.

If you are investing in the rental business, your tenants are your primary source of income, so make them your priority. The rent generated from your property serves as a consistent cash flow for investing in real estate. To keep it up, ensure your tenants are happy and satisfied with your services.

Attend to complaints promptly and come up with policies that will be beneficial to your tenants.

2. A Property Manager will do the trick.

Property management has been discussed in a previous chapter, and you can recall the forms of property management discussed. As a beginner in the real estate business, self-management was recommended. Now that there are many properties to look after, it is safe to say a property manager will do the trick.

Recruit a competent and reliable property manager or caretaker. A property management company can also be beneficial, drop ending on your wants and resources. This will save you the stress and hassle of managing several properties.

3. Manage and maintain your properties.

The most important method of keeping your investments is to manage and maintain your properties. This is how you can increase the value of your property and attract your desired clients. Maintenance is critical and can go a long way in generating sustainable wealth in your real estate investments.

Make improvements to your property where necessary and boost its features. Conversions are good, rehabilitation, and renovations are even better.

5. Insurance protects your properties.

One sure way to ensure you don't lose much as a real estate investor is INSURANCE. Avoid losses from natural disasters, accidents, and litigation by insuring your properties. Invest in a reliable insurance company with a great offer. Ignorance is deadly; insurance is reviving!

6. Put your investments under a corporation.

To reduce liability and to ensure the protection of your properties, you should invest in a corporation.

Register your investments under LLC and be assured of little or no liability.

7. Know when to call it quits.

While you can leverage on debt to acquire properties at a lower price to their original market price, it's best if you are careful. If not careful, you may acquire an investment with too many debt payments. Know when to use leverage to your advantage and know when to call it quits.

9. Prepare an "Exit Strategy."

With every investment deal you secure, there must be an exit strategy for when you decide to opt out. Always have an exit strategy ready to be executed as soon as you give the signal. Review the different exit strategies available and choose the one that's suitable for the deal at hand.

11. Face issues of cash flow squarely.

There are times when problems may arise in regards to your cash flows; to protect your investments, face them squarely. Take bold steps and measures to ensure that the challenges are solved and you are back on track.

12. Work with the local authorities

To ensure the smooth running of your real estate business, it is imperative you work with the local authorities. Know the various organisations available in that locality and ensure you create a strong rapport with their representatives.

Visit the local government to learn more about the vicinity and how you can increase the value of your property.

It is essential you know how to keep your investments safe and not fall victim of fraud, scam, or bankruptcy. Don't lose your wealth; instead generate more!

Conclusion

As an adult who pays the bills, you need not be worried about how to earn more and become wealthy. You need to step up your game and actualise your dreams. You have been given a seed of knowledge; sow it well and reap the abundant fruits of sustainable wealth.

You have reached the end of the book and hopefully you enjoyed what you read. Now, you may be wondering what's next. This is what's next; take ACTION and achieve your dreams of creating sustainable wealth through real estate investments.

Since you now understand that real estate is a pathway to sustainable wealth and you have a great asset (this book) to see you through, you can proceed toward actualising your dreams. Don't forget to avoid the 'get-rich-quick" approach and exercise patience in order to succeed. Numerous ways to build wealth in real estate have been discussed. Now, you can work toward building your business and wealth.

Starting up in real estate isn't simple, especially if you are a beginner. With the tips learned on raising money, you will be fine. Once you start investing properly, don't forget to handle your real estate investments as a business. This will lead you to defensive investing and the principles learned in this book will serve as a guide.

Having a consistent cash flow is important in running your real estate business, so, manage it well with all you learned in this book. Securing an investment deal requires 'closing' money. You are well equipped on how to raise your 'closing' money. With a goal of achieving sustainable wealth through real estate investments, increasing the value of your property is inevitable; make it count.

Practice the several methods learned to invest for maximum gain. If you are aspiring to become a landlord, you have learned the ways to become a successful landlord and keep your tenants happy and satisfied.

A lucrative investment deal should be accompanied by an exit strategy, or several exit strategies, depending on what you aim to achieve. No one is immune to investment scams, you can only be careful enough to not fall victim. When you eventually get what you want, keep it well.

Financial freedom can be yours; all you need do is to implement all you have learned in this book. With persistent effort and patience, you will gain it!

***

www.ingramcontent.com/pod-product-compliance
Lightning Source LLC
Chambersburg PA
CBHW071711210326
41597CB00017B/2435